THE EMERALD QUEEN

sed on the blessed Blooms of the Garden writings.

Other books about Princess Kaylee Marie are:

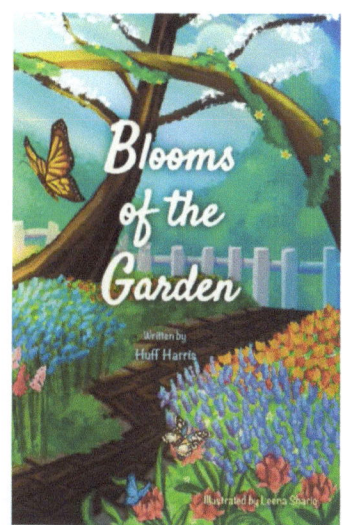 

Huff & Harris

Copyright @ 2023 Huff Harris LLC

Ba

This book is dedicated to Queen Cecelia Howard, our mother, as we celebrate and honor her on the 80th milestone of life, love, and legacy.

EXODUS 20:12

"Honor your father and your mother, that your days may be long upon the land which the Lord your God is giving you."

At bedtime, Princess Kaylee grabbed a book for her daddy to read. The book was about the Emerald Queen.

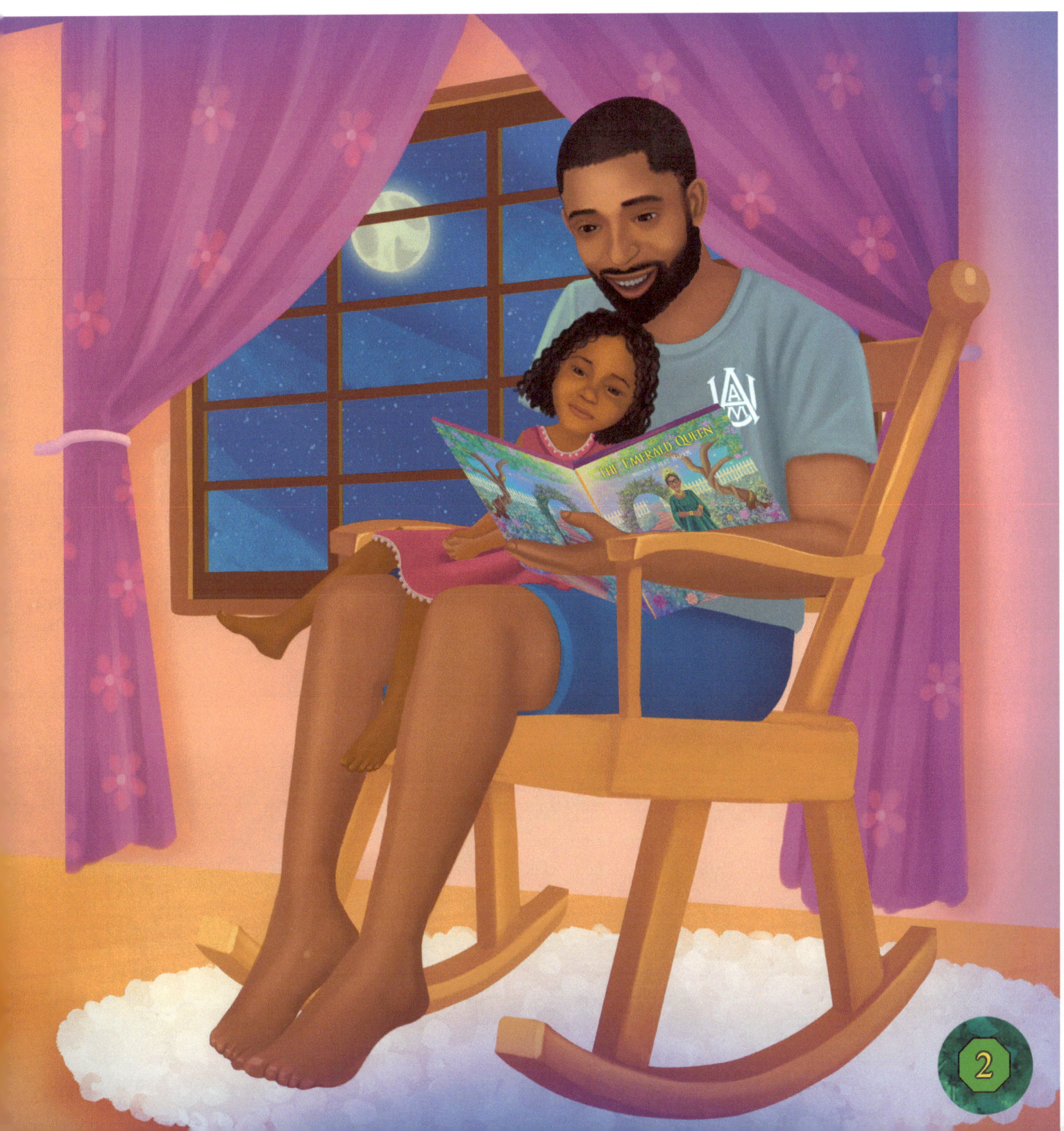

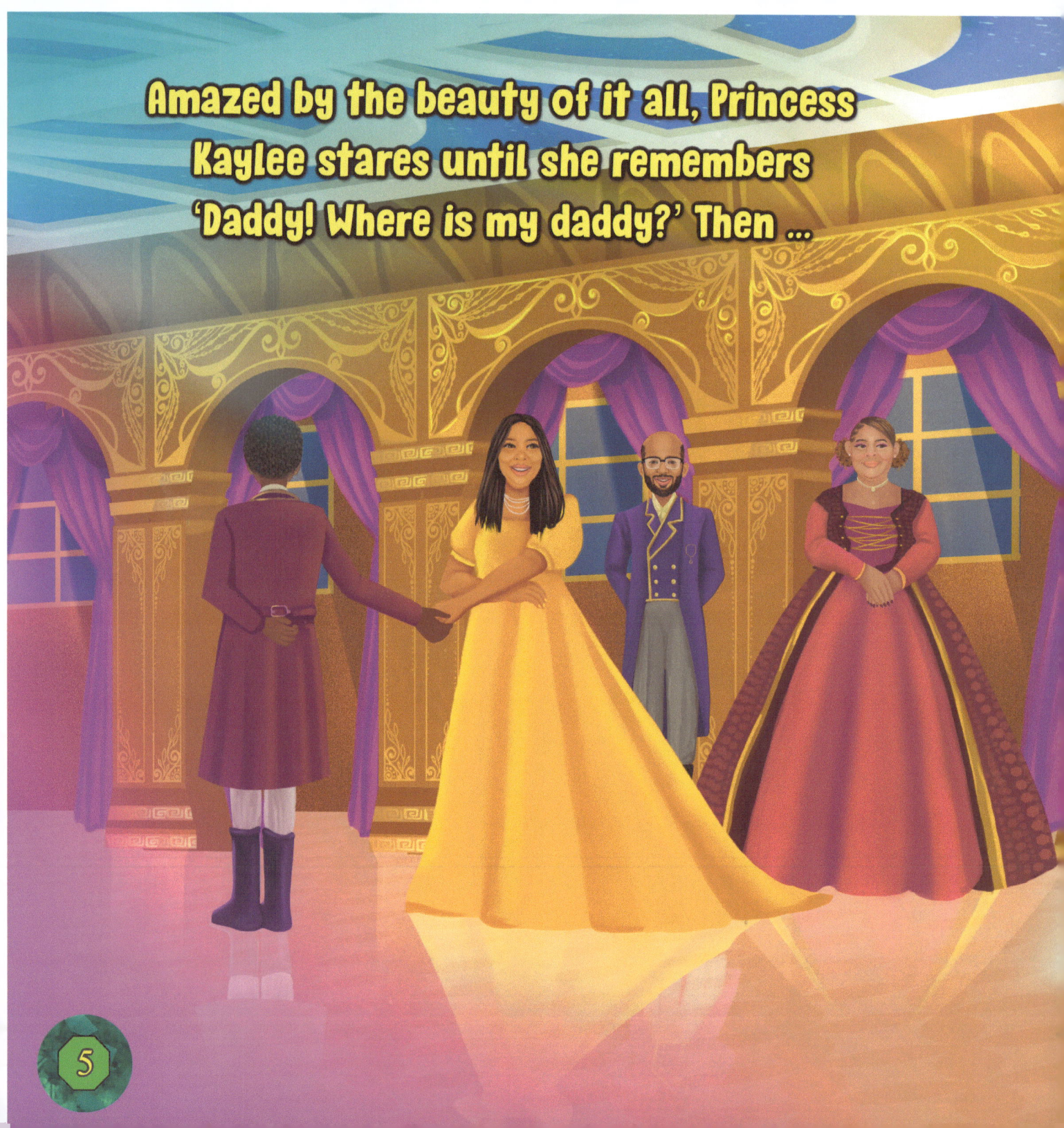

Amazed by the beauty of it all, Princess Kaylee stares until she remembers 'Daddy! Where is my daddy?' Then ...

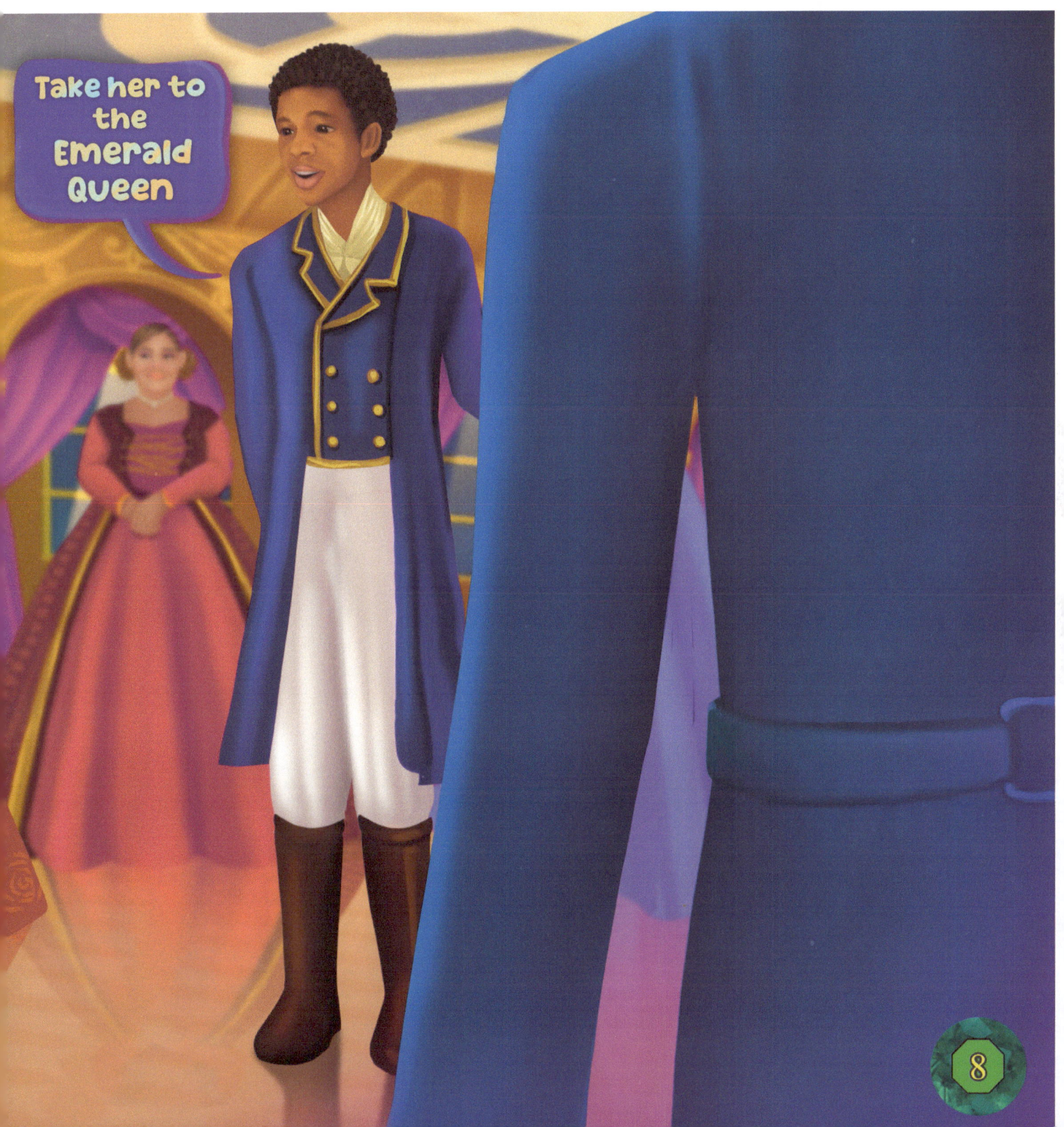

Overwhelmed and unable to find her father, Princess Kaylee begins to cry.

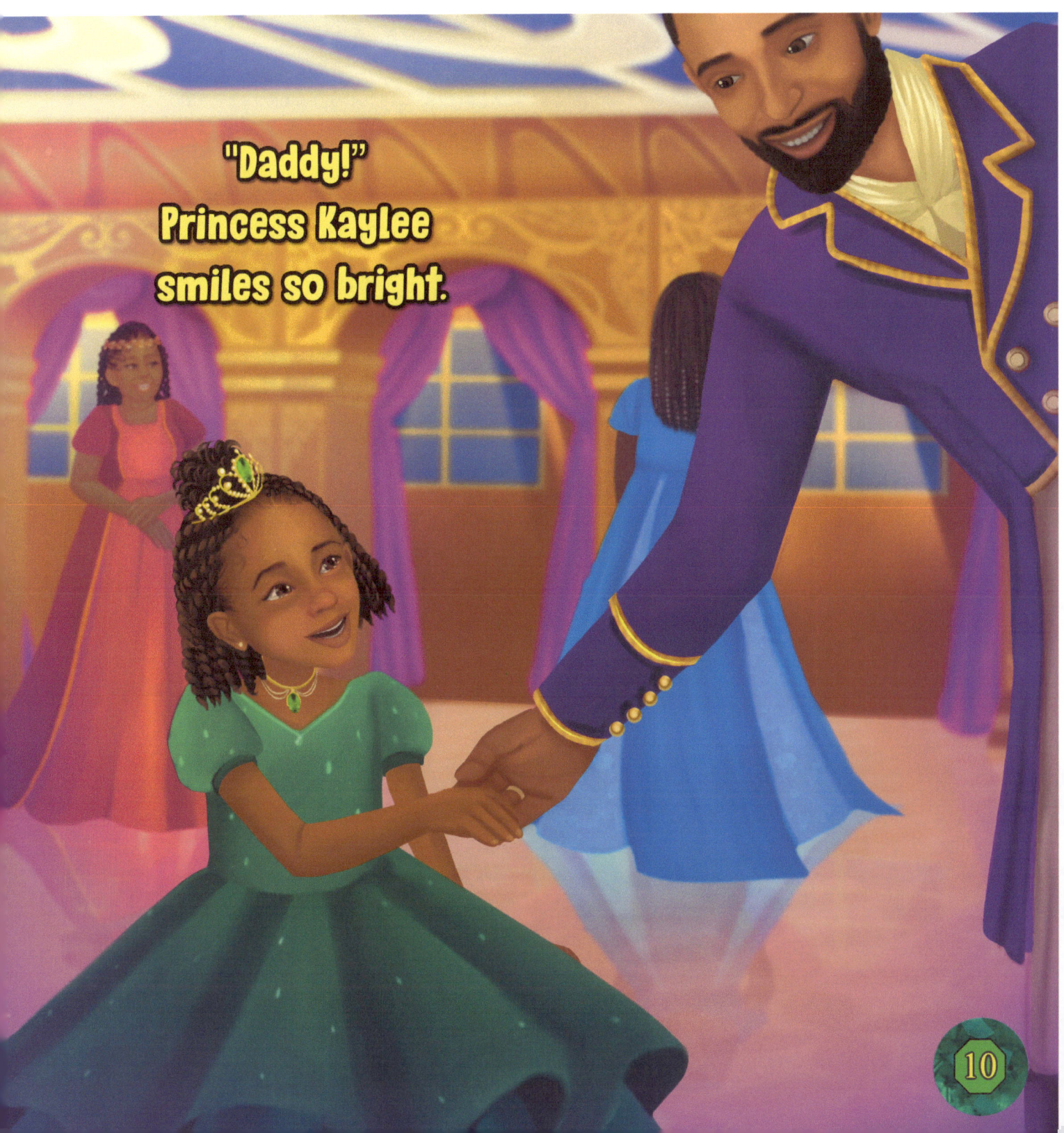

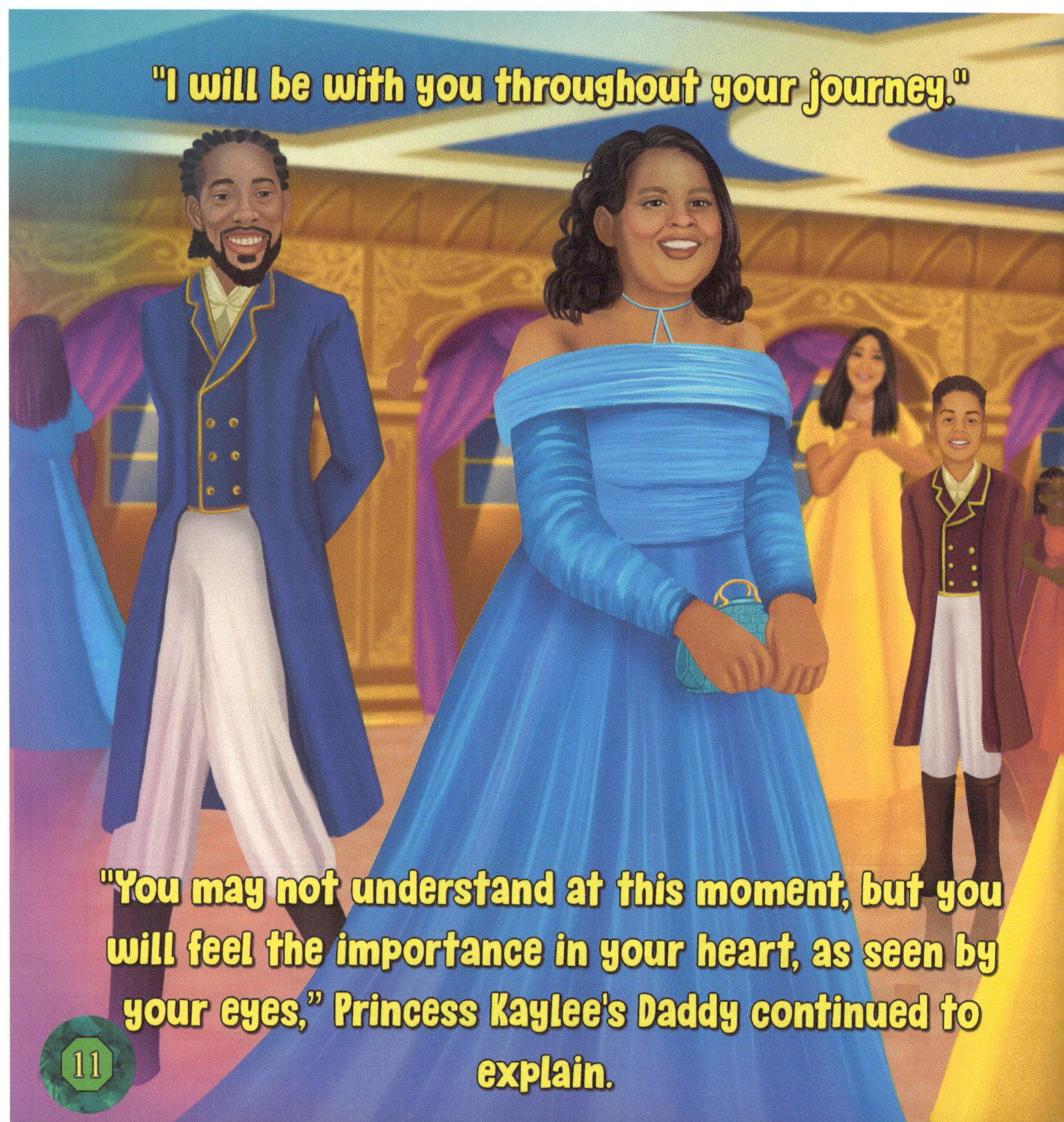

"I will be with you throughout your journey."

"You may not understand at this moment, but you will feel the importance in your heart, as seen by your eyes," Princess Kaylee's Daddy continued to explain.

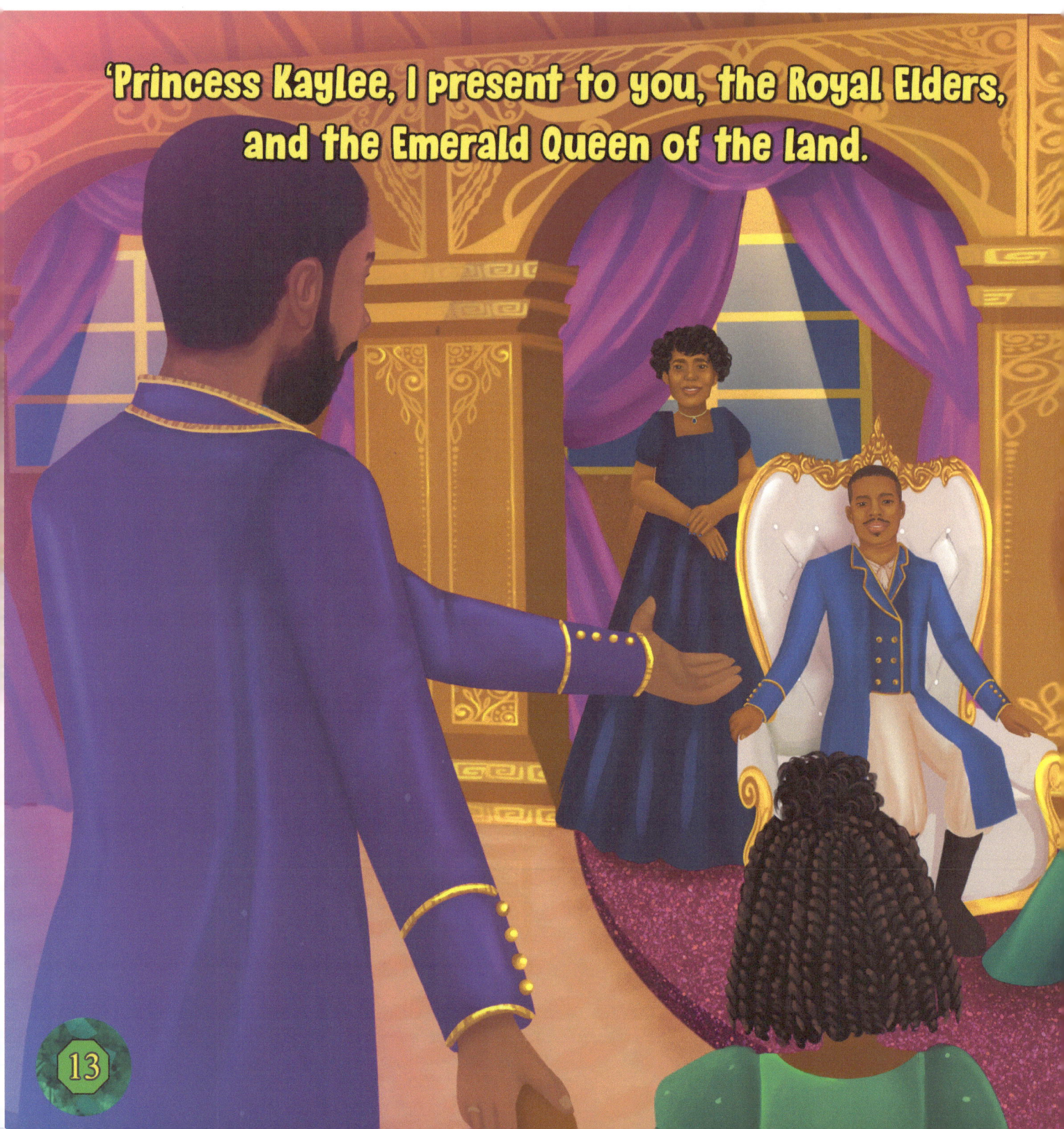

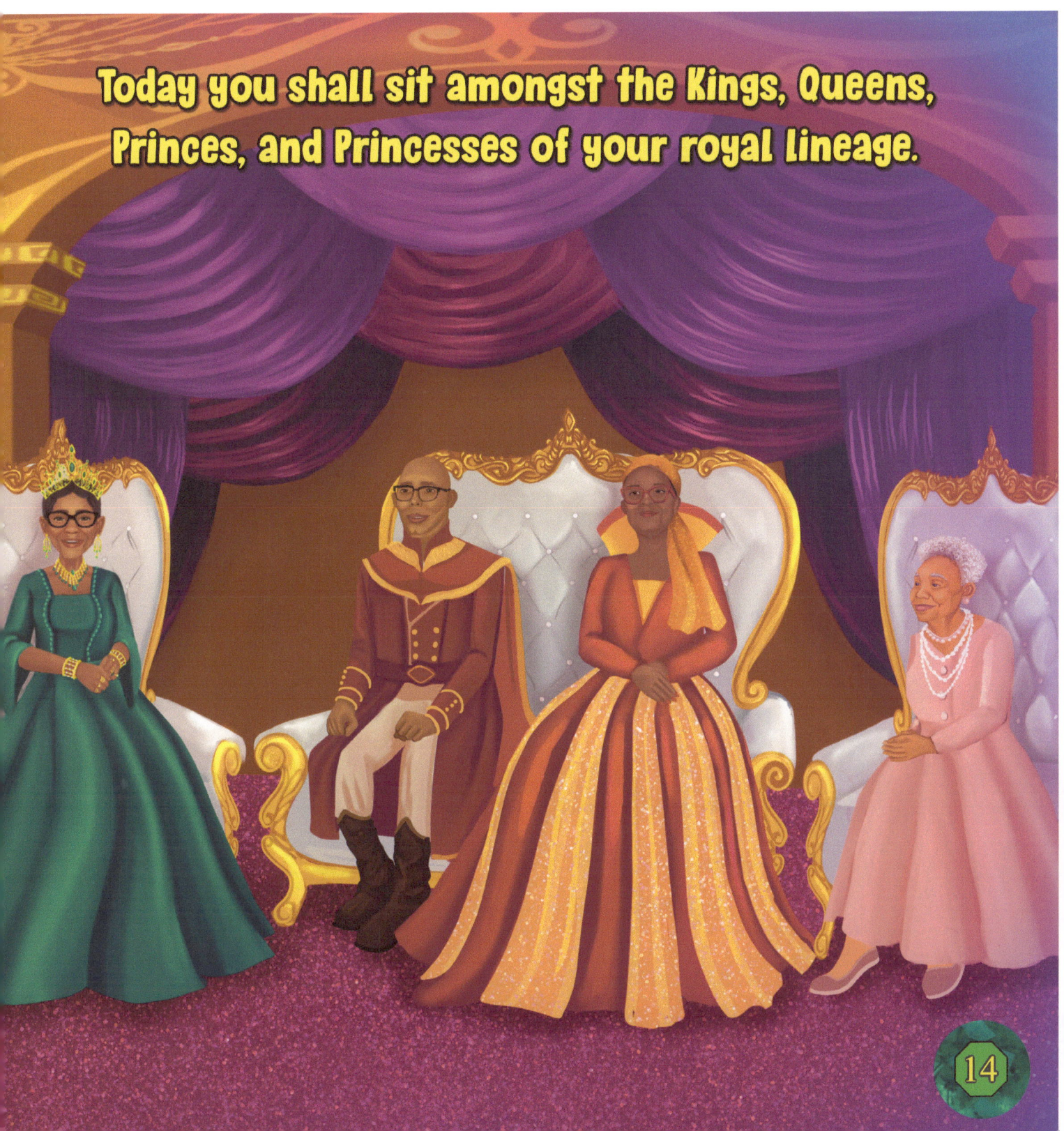
Today you shall sit amongst the Kings, Queens, Princes, and Princesses of your royal lineage.

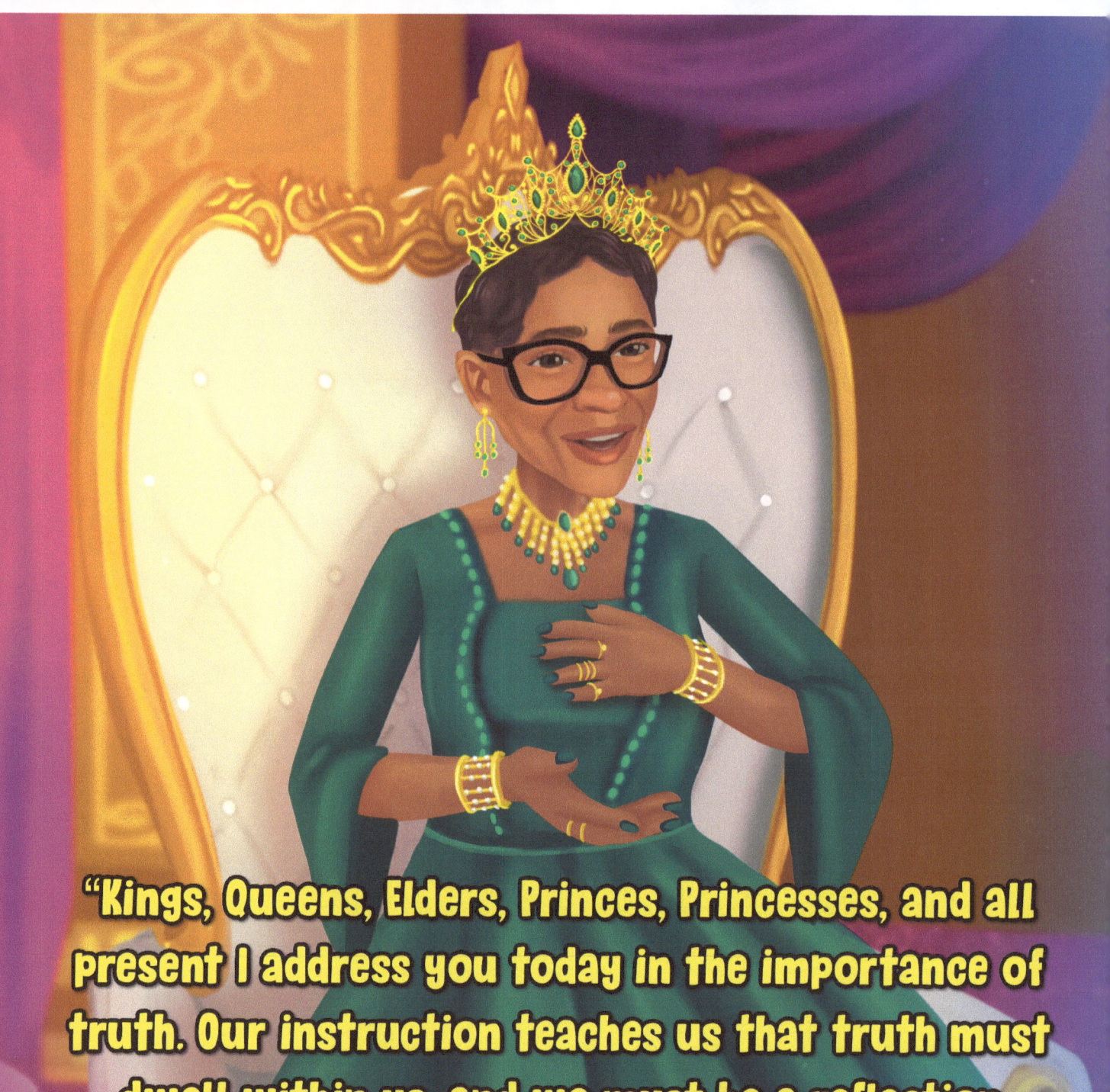

"Kings, Queens, Elders, Princes, Princesses, and all present I address you today in the importance of truth. Our instruction teaches us that truth must dwell within us, and we must be a reflection of IT (TRUTH)."

Let Truth Abide in You, 1 John 2:24-27

Therefore, let that abide in you which you heard from the beginning. If what you heard from the beginning abides in you, you also will abide in the Son and in the Father. And this is the promise that He has promised us eternal life.

These things I have written to you concerning those who try to deceive you. But the anointing which you have received from Him abides in you, and you do not need that anyone teach you; but as the same anointing teaches you concerning all things, and is true, and is not a lie, and just as it has taught you, you will aide in Him.

The Emerald Queen addresses the Kings, Queens, Princes, Princesses, and all present. "Just as the truth lives in you, believe in it, live it, reflect it, walk it, and seek from it... the truth, my loved ones, the truth.

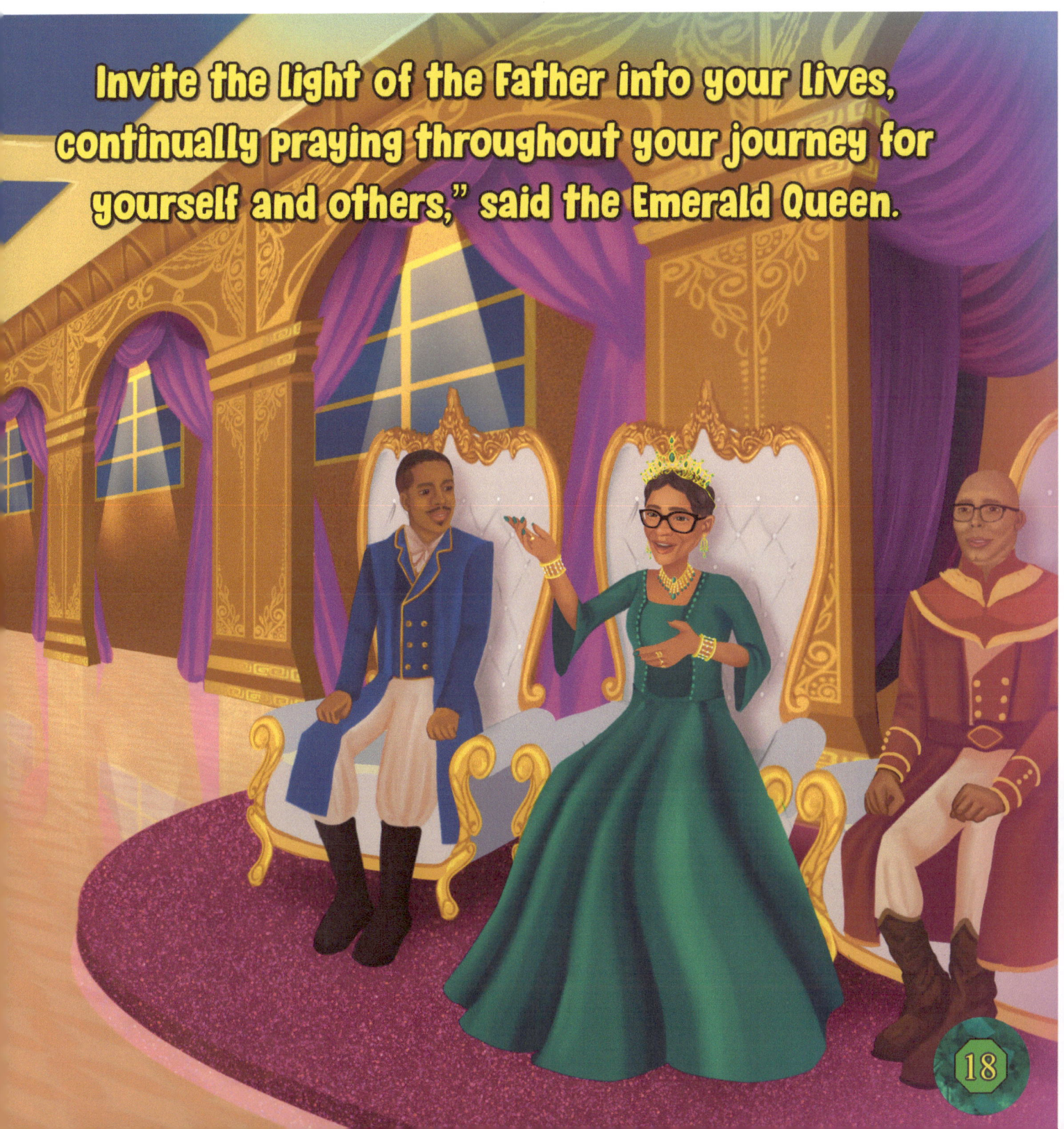

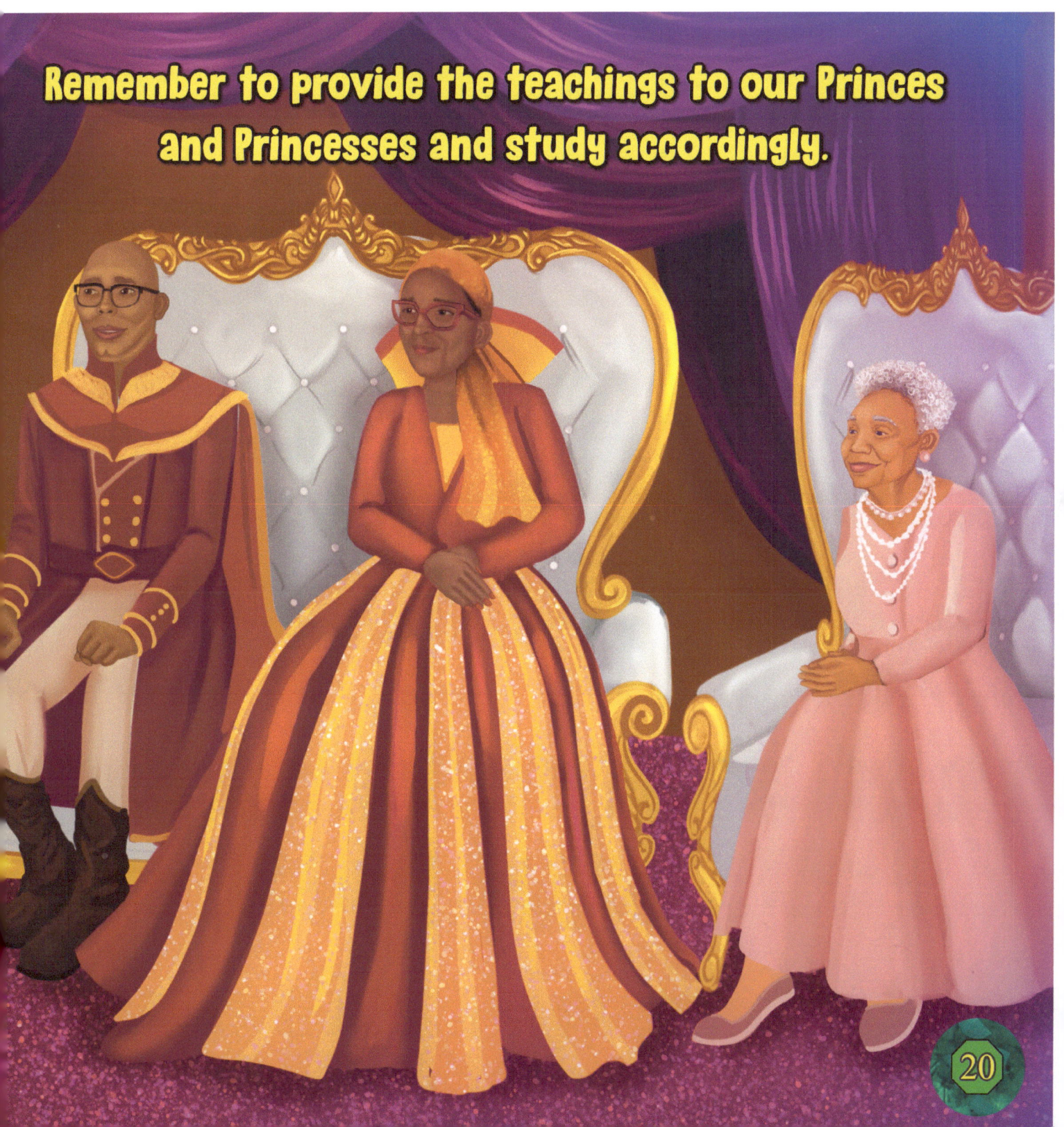

"The Word of Instruction has guided me through my eighty-year journey," said the Emerald Queen.

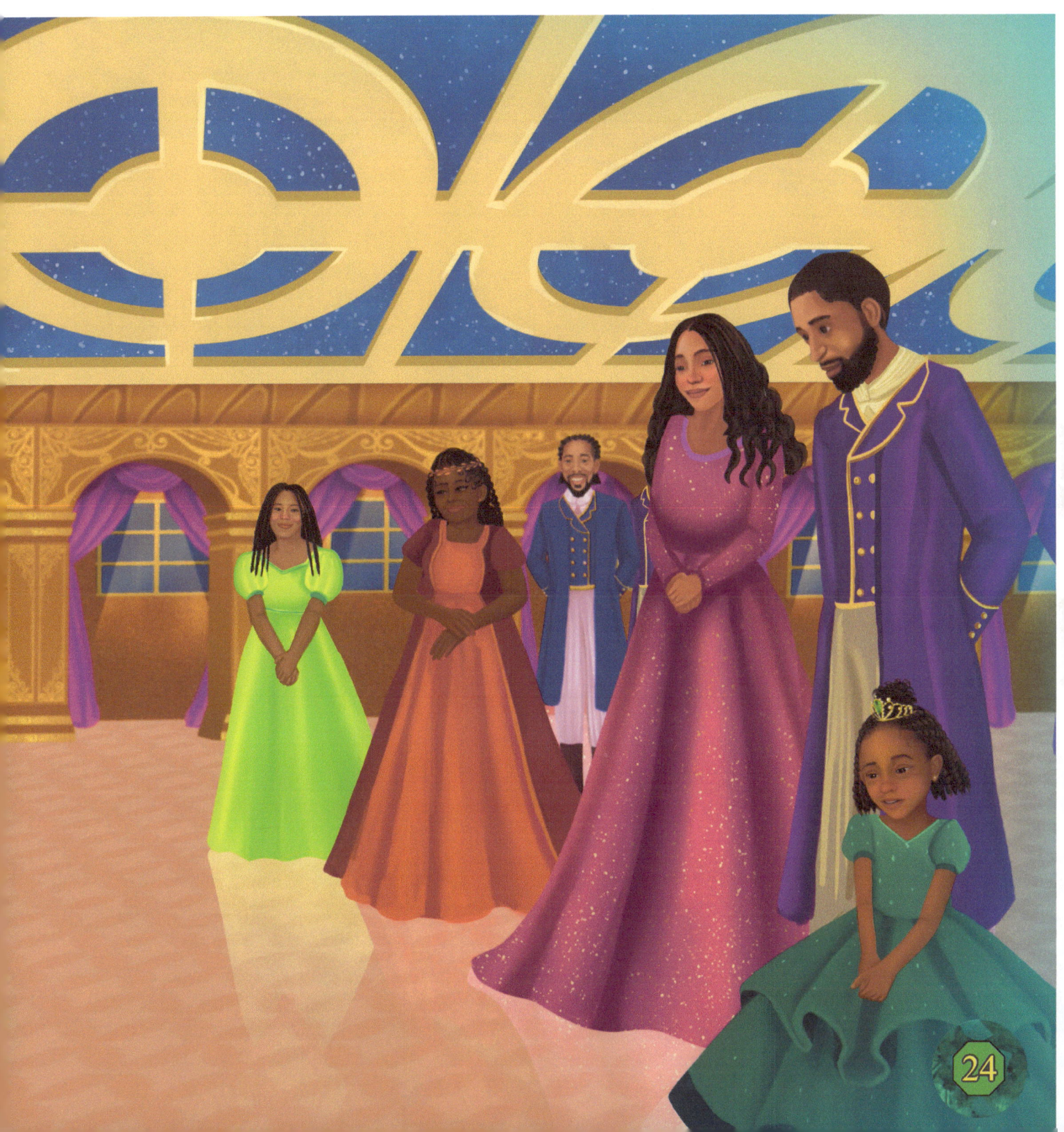

Prayer of the Emerald Queen

Father of our Lord, Jesus Christ,
from whom the whole family in heaven and earth is named.
Our King, Our Shepherd, Our Everything! As we humble ourselves before you, we ask for your forgiveness of deed, thought, or act that was or is unlike you and not acceptable in Thine sight.
We utter thanksgiving to You for Your Son and the Holy Spirit, the Trinity.
We further thank you for this time to gather, of planting, to build up, to embrace, for the gain, and this time to love.

As we go forth on our separate journeys, and as Christ may dwell in our hearts through faith, remaining rooted in your big garden and nourished in love — comprehending with all the saints what is the width and length and depth and height knowing the love of Christ which passes knowledge, that we may be filled with all the fullness of You, God our Father.
You, the One who is able to do exceedingly abundantly of above all things asked or thought of, according to the power working in us.
To You, the glory of church by Christ Jesus to all the generations before us, forever and ever. Amen

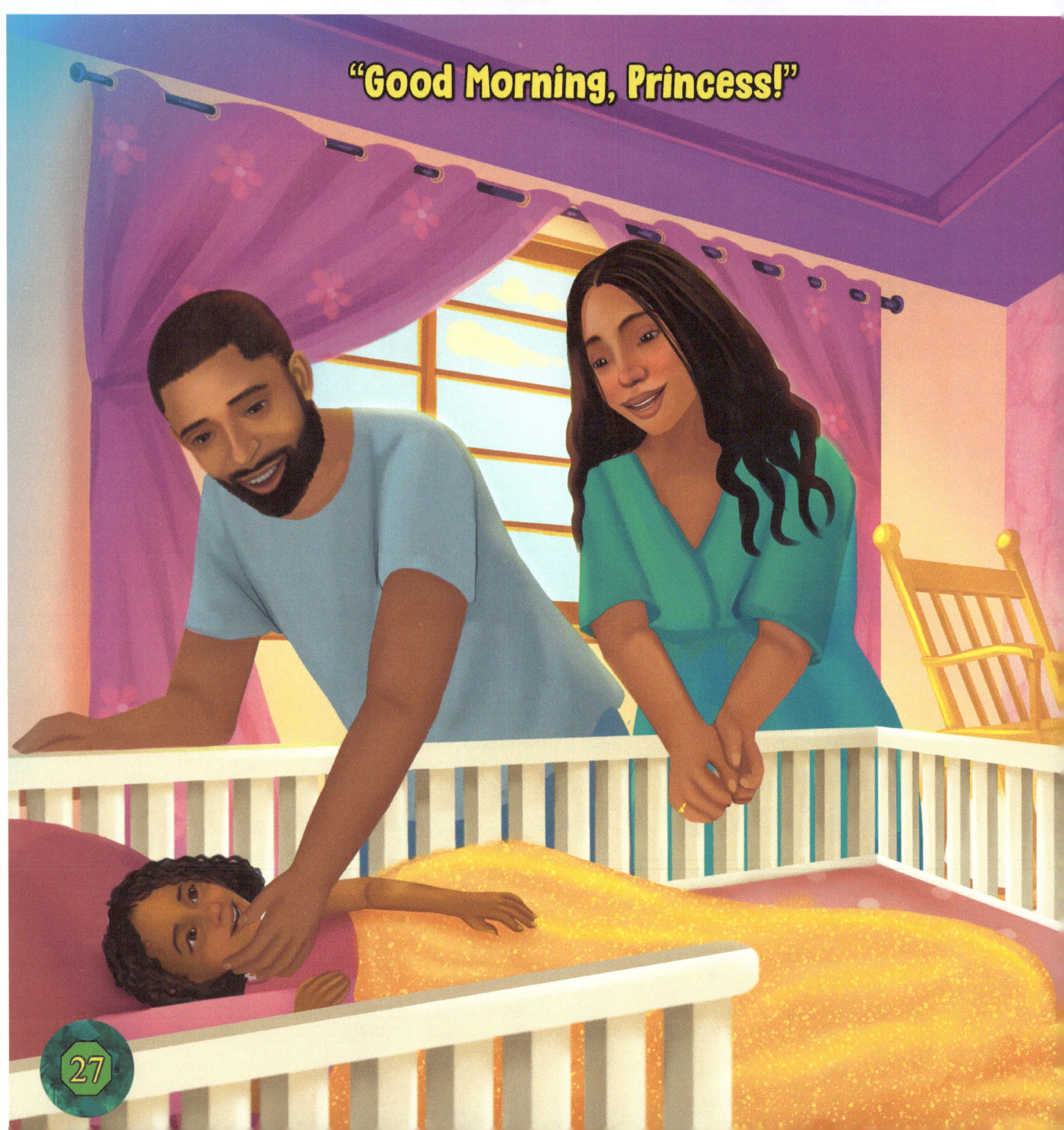

Huff Harris are the loving grandparents of Kaylee Marie. They are blessed by the life and curiosity of their Princess while making it a priority to teach her in accordance with the Word.

This is the third book on little Kaylee's adventures, journey, and teachings. The inspiration to write about Kaylee was whispered into her grandmother's heart by a higher being.

OTHER BOOKS ABOUT
PRINCESS KAYLEE MARIE ARE:
The Blooms of the Garden
The First Bloom Goes Home

Copyright @ 2023 Huff Harris LLC

www.ingramcontent.com/pod-product-compliance
Lightning Source LLC
LaVergne TN
LVHW070434080526
838201LV00132B/270